It isn't good · to keep things · bottled up

DRINK WINE

A Coloring Book For Wine Lovers

This book belongs to:

_____

_____

This book has been designed for coloring. Be as creative and colorful as you like — technicolor is good! Each coloring page has a framed blank page on its flip side to use as you wish — doodling, journaling, sketching, wine thoughts — or anything else you can think of.

Enjoy!

I Prefer My GRapes Crushed And In A GlasS

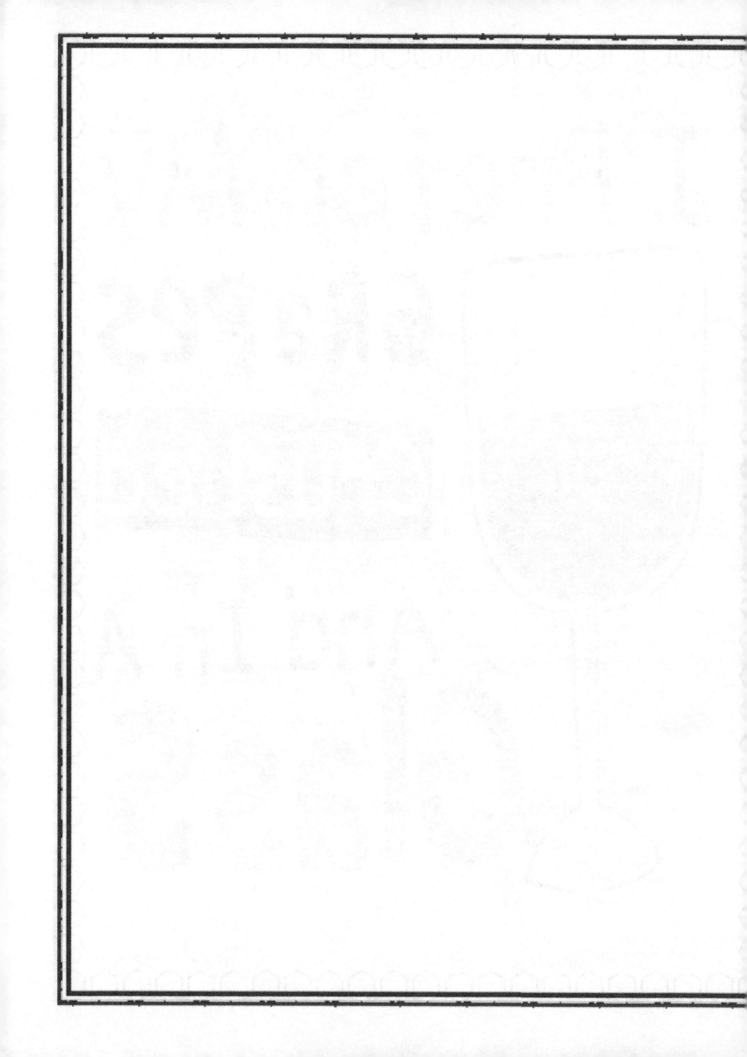

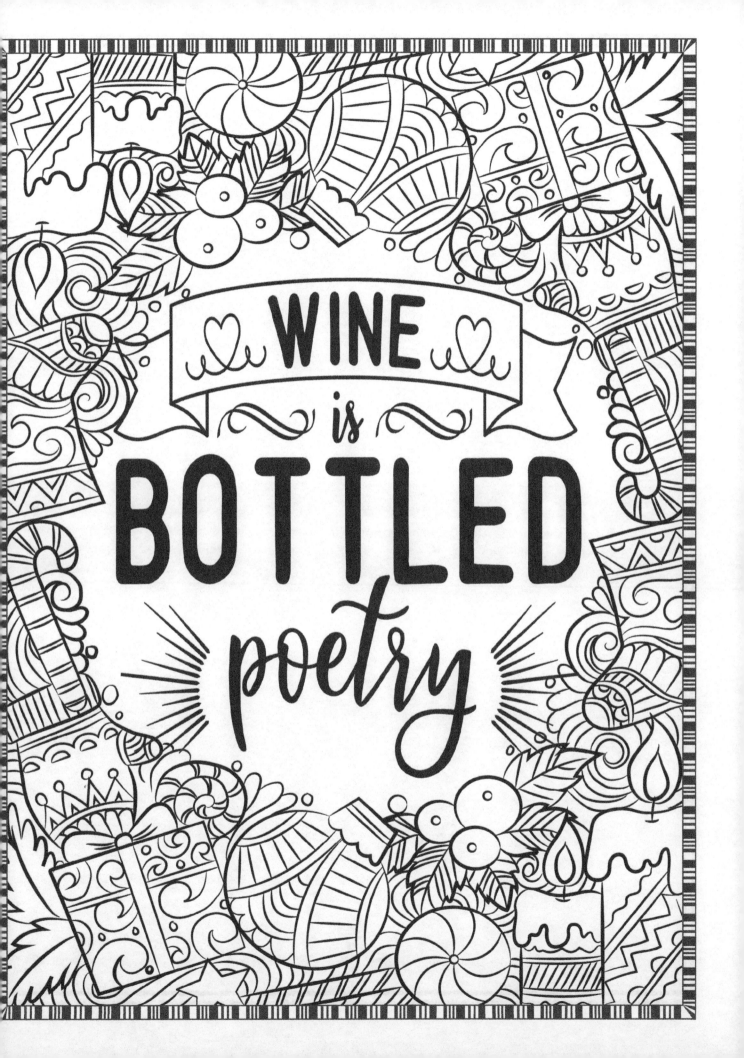

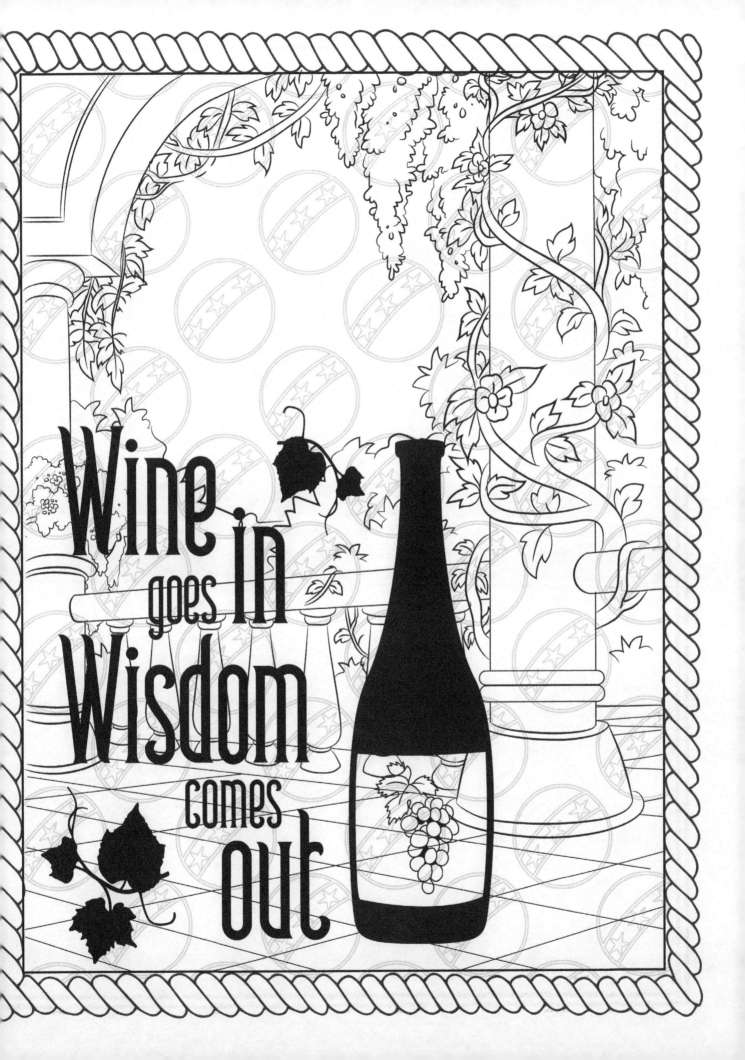

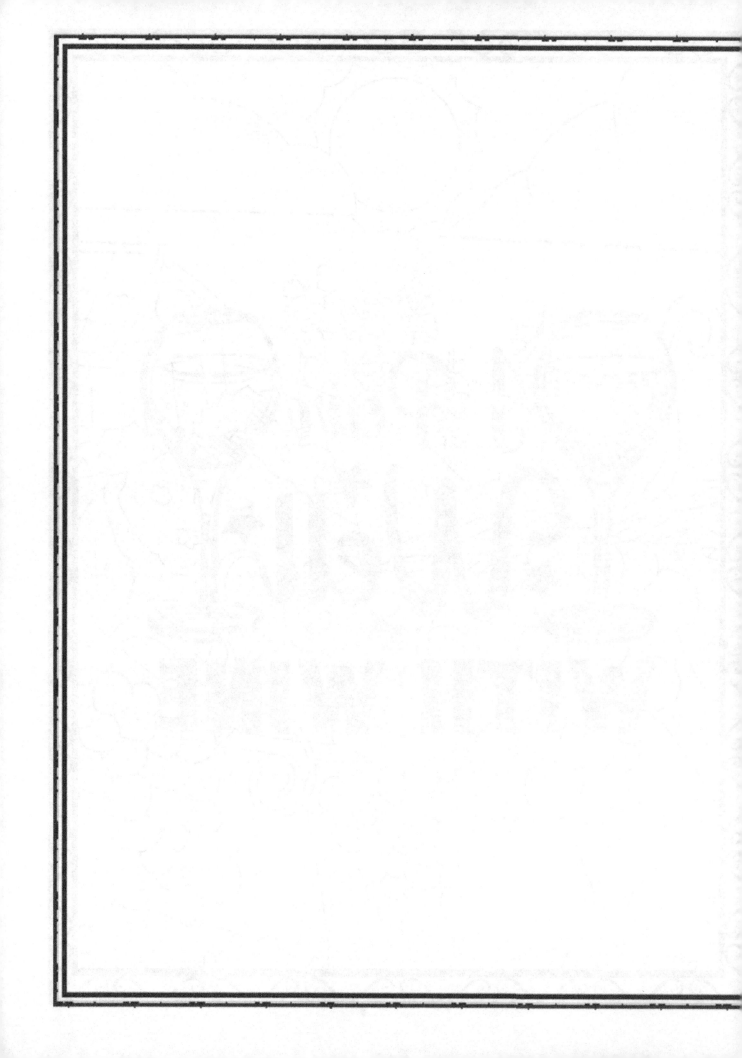

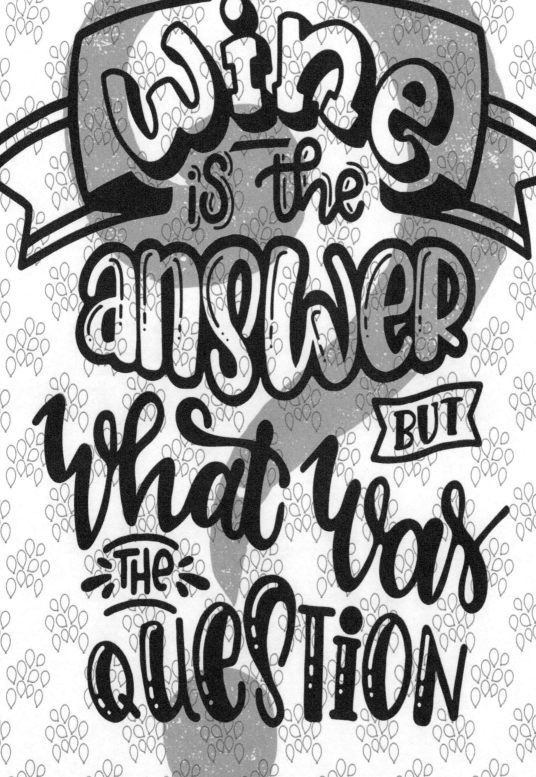

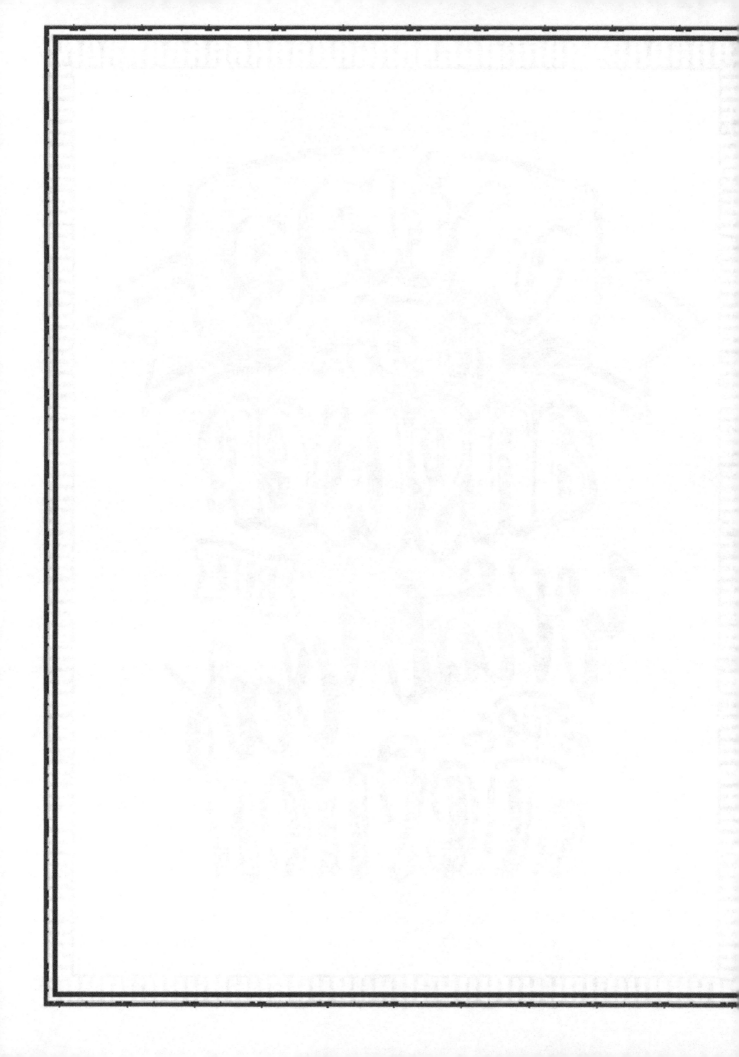

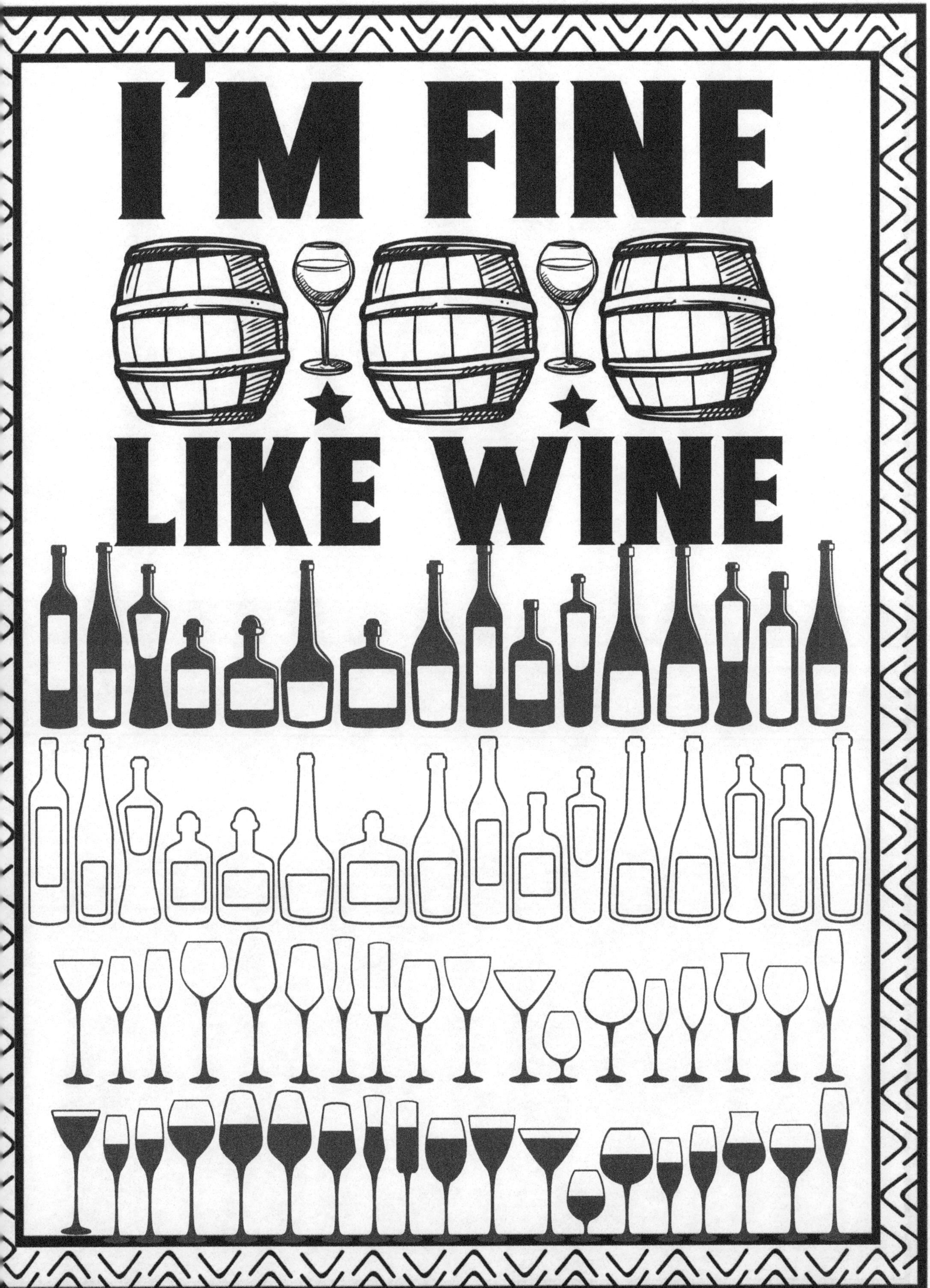
I'M FINE
LIKE WINE

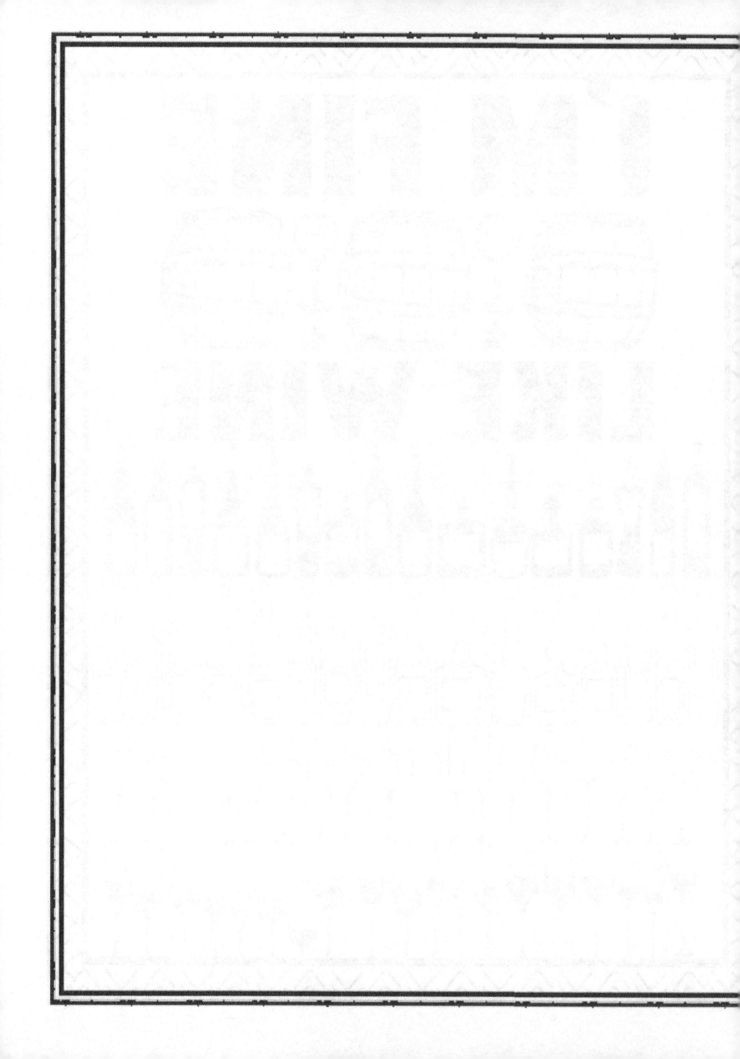

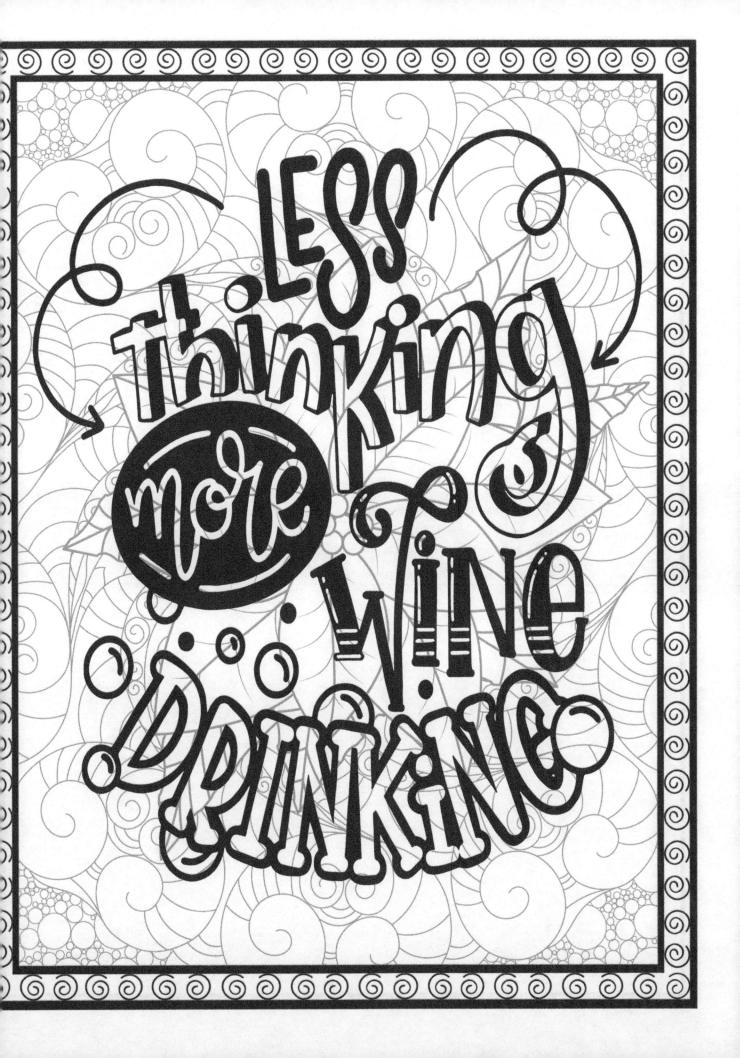

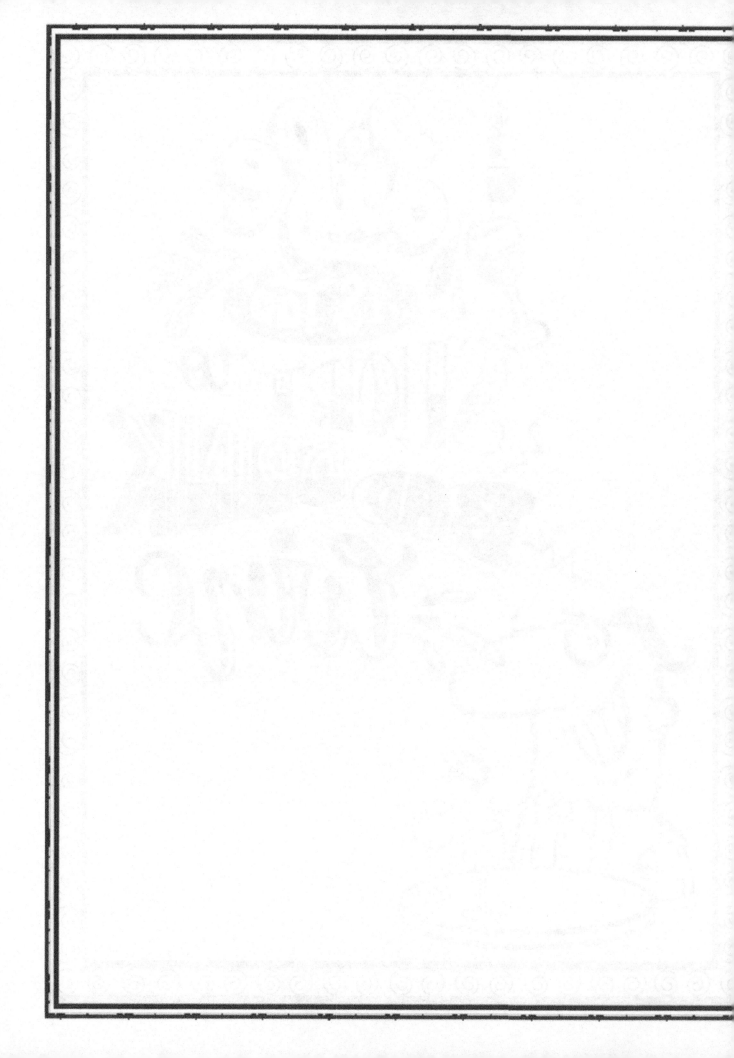

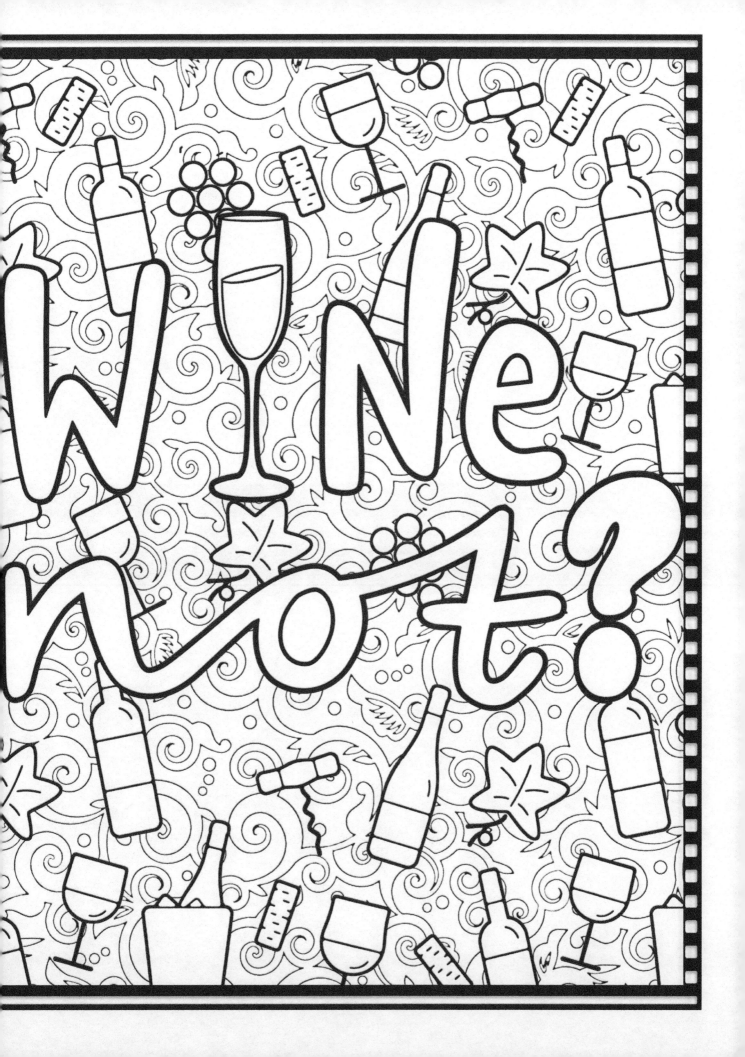

The best
wines
ARE THE ONES WE
drink
WITH FRIENDS

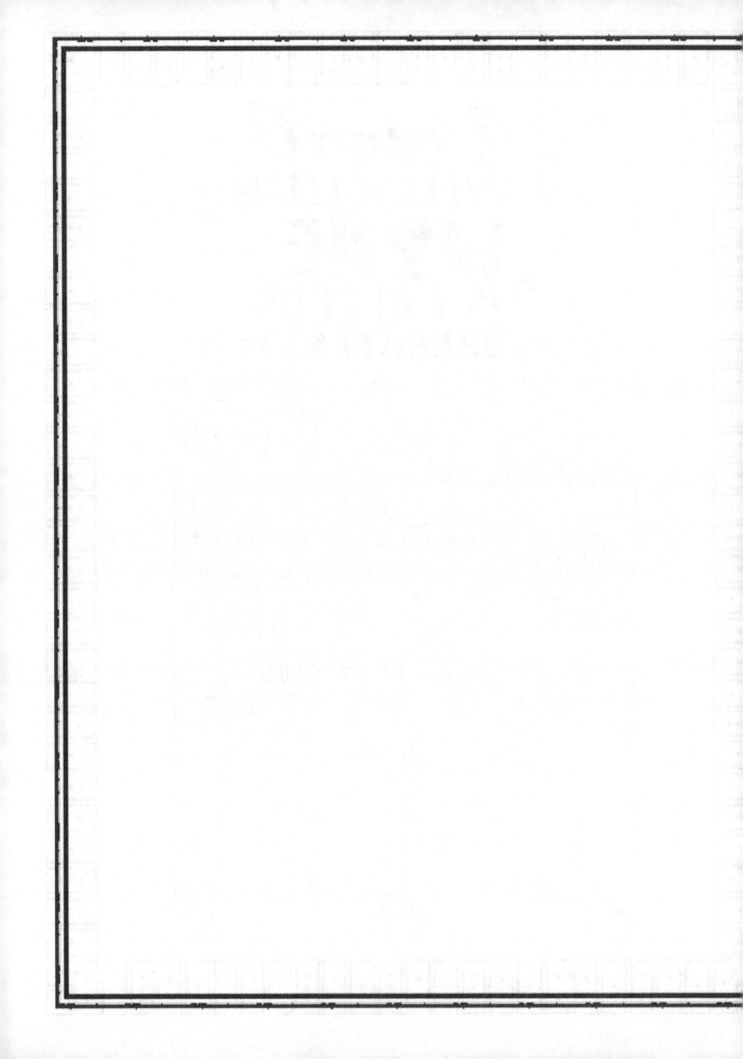

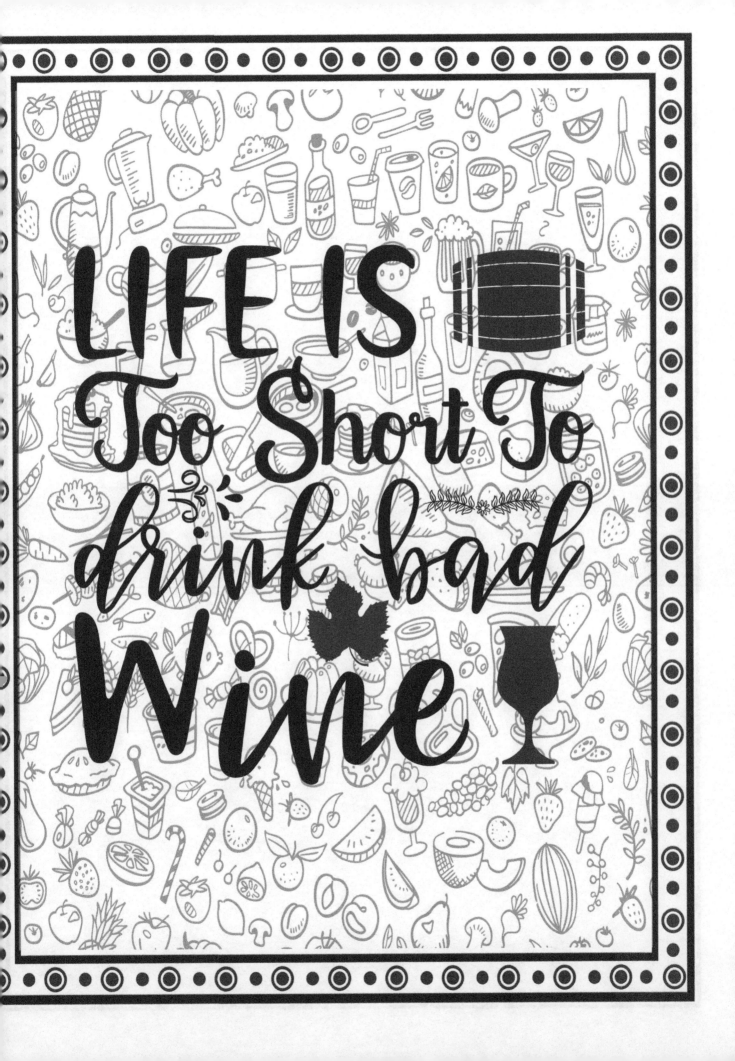

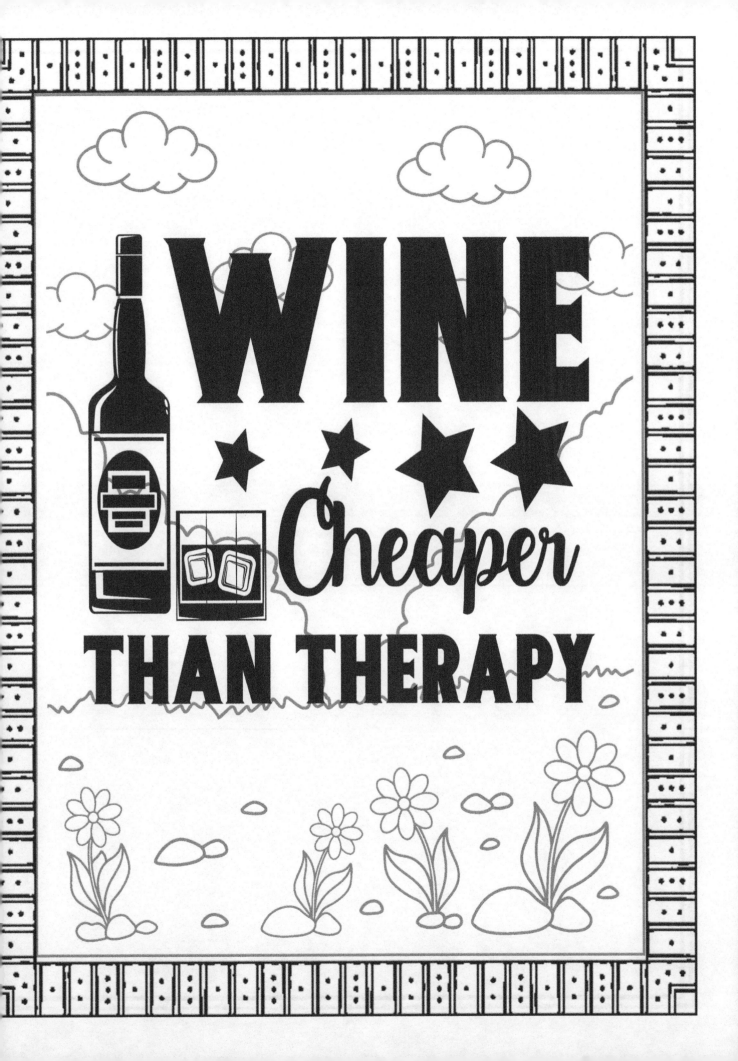

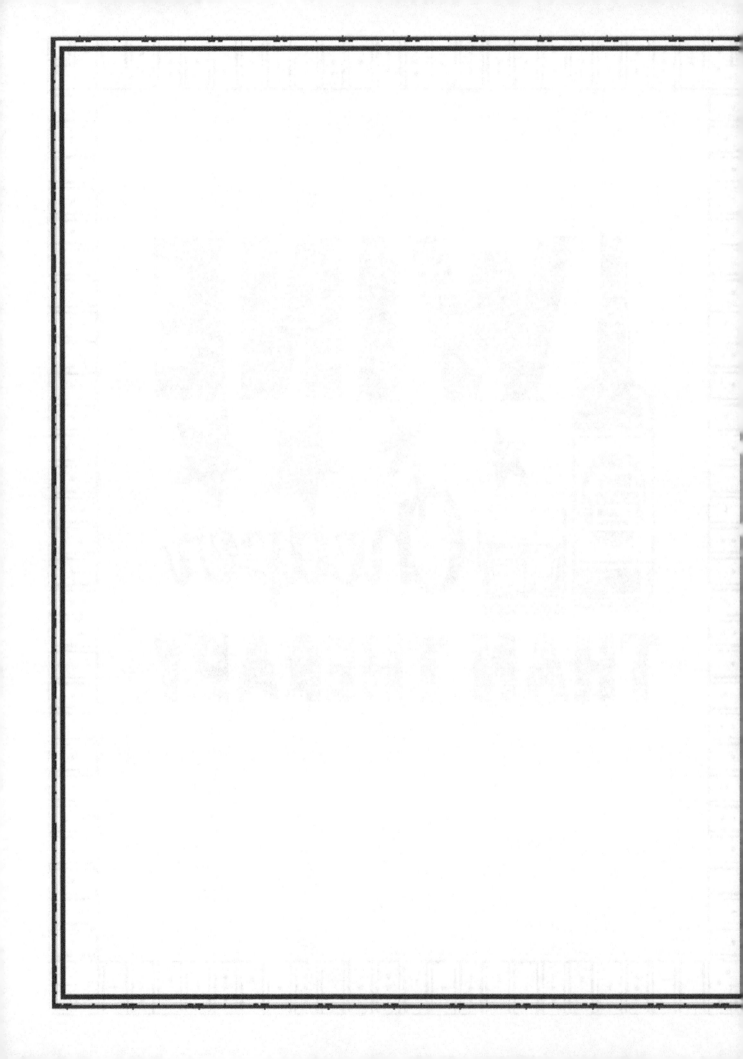

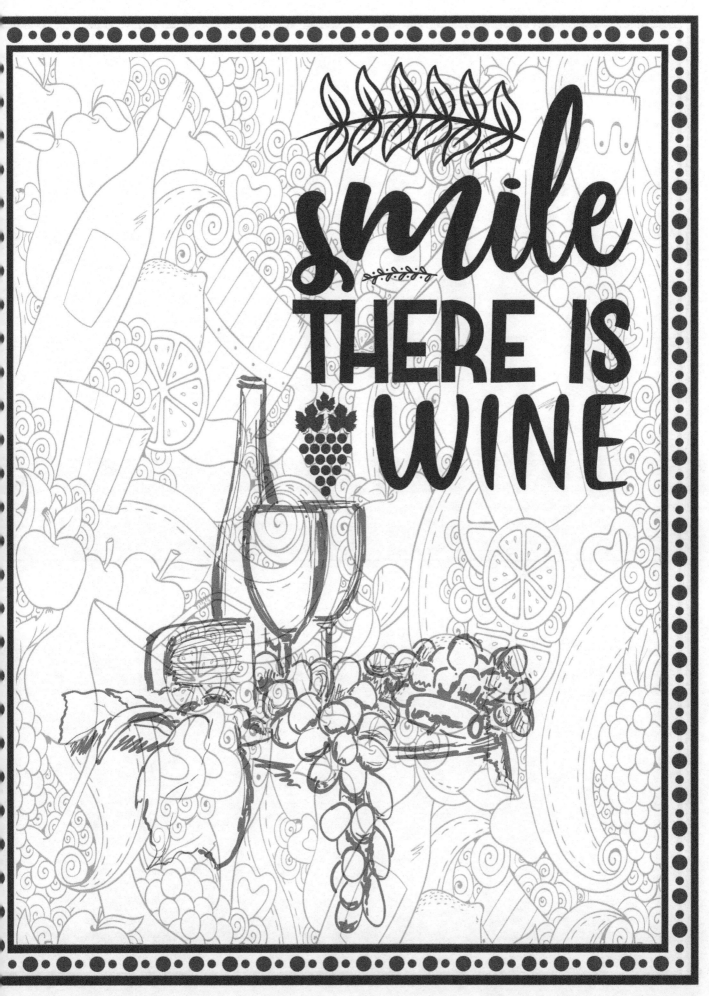

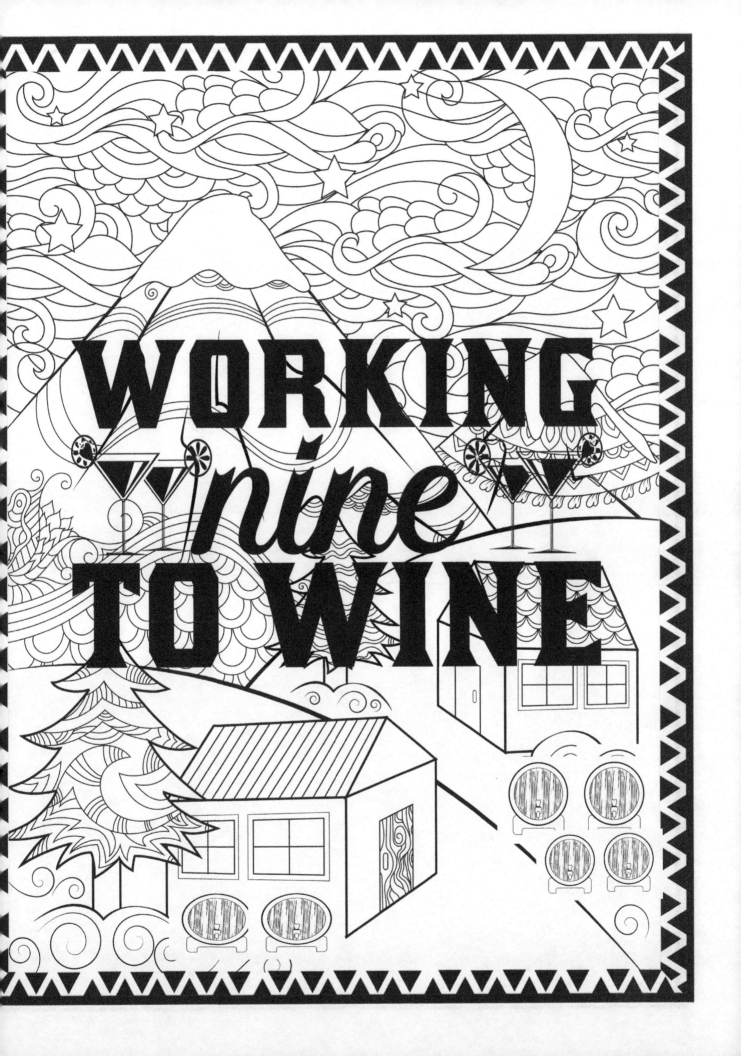

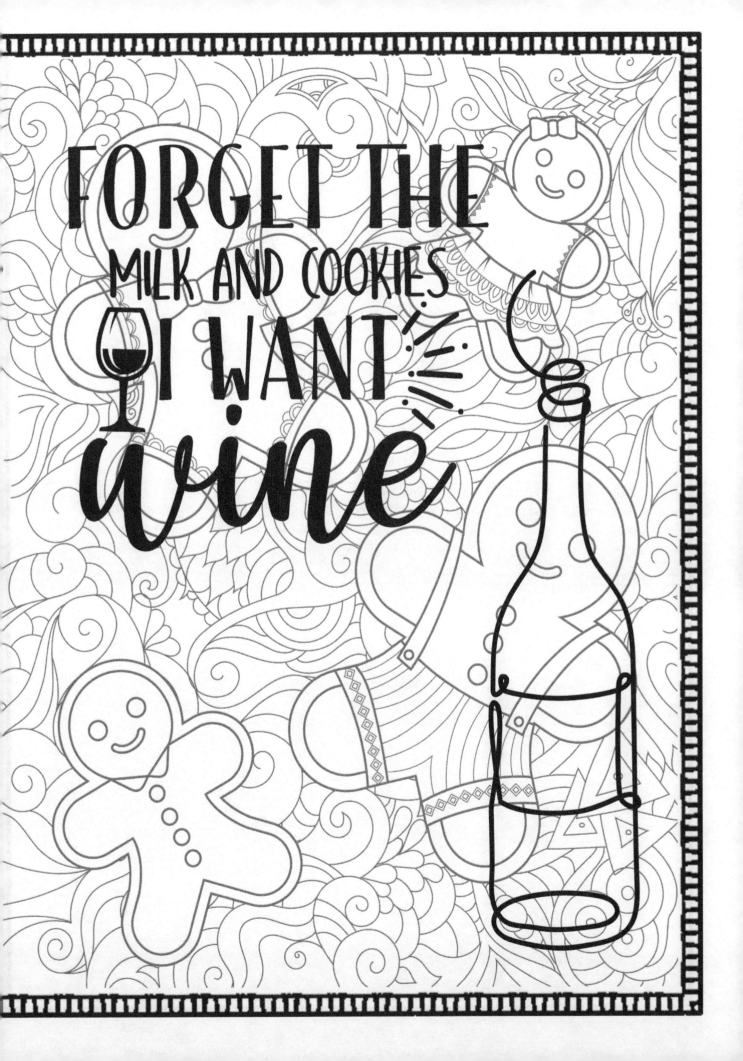

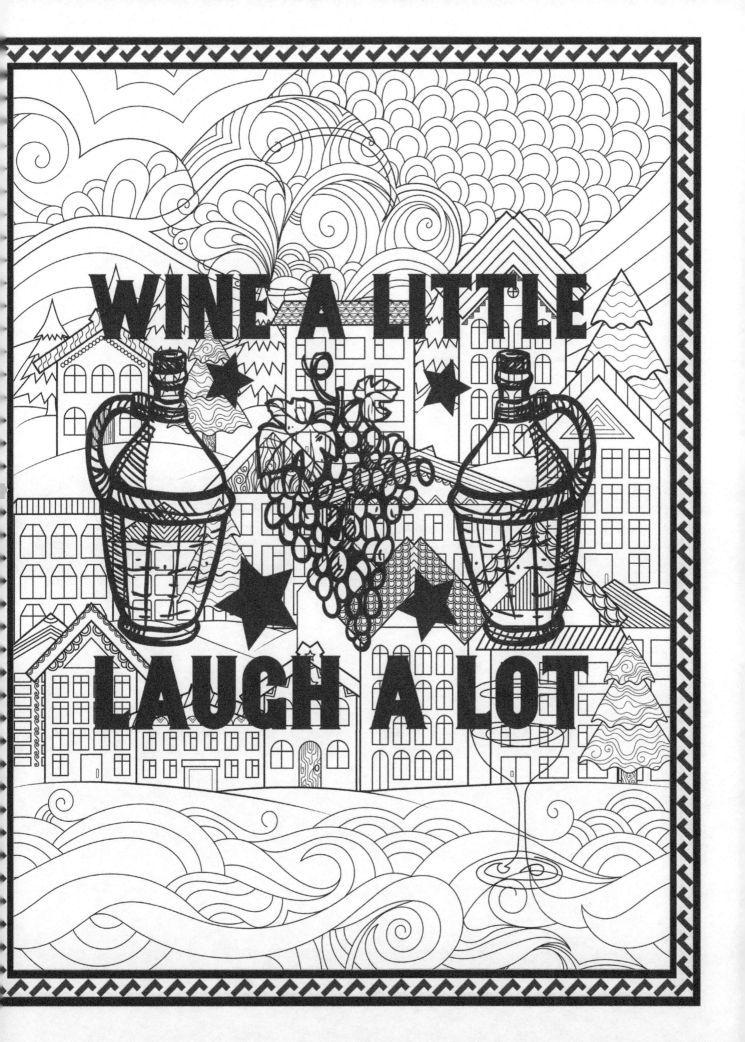

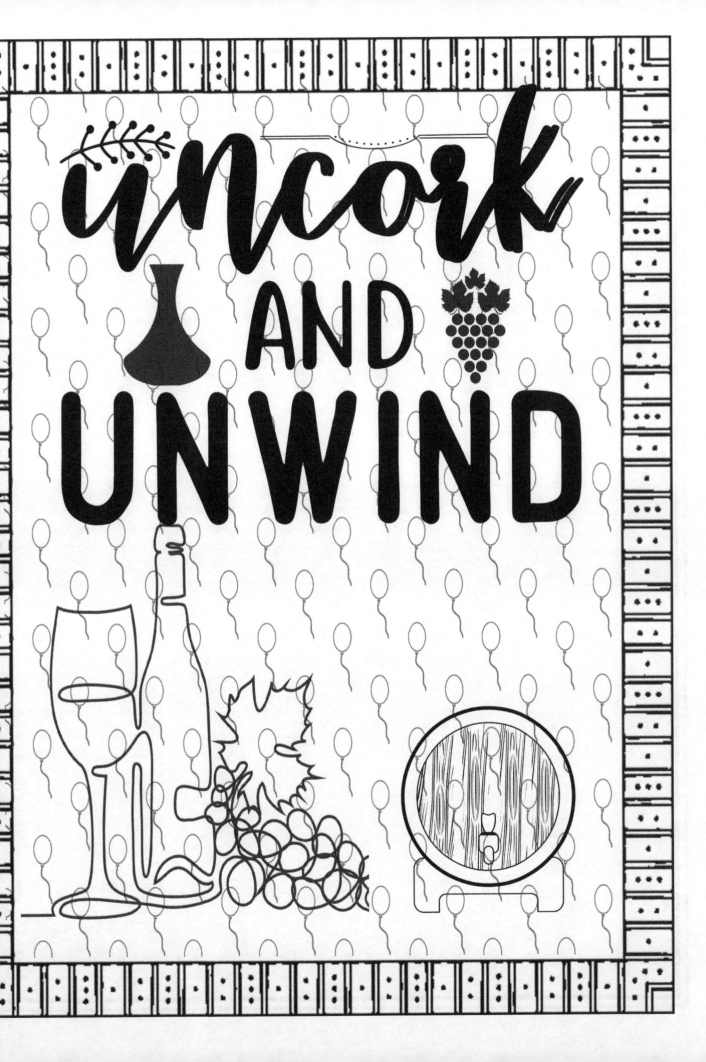

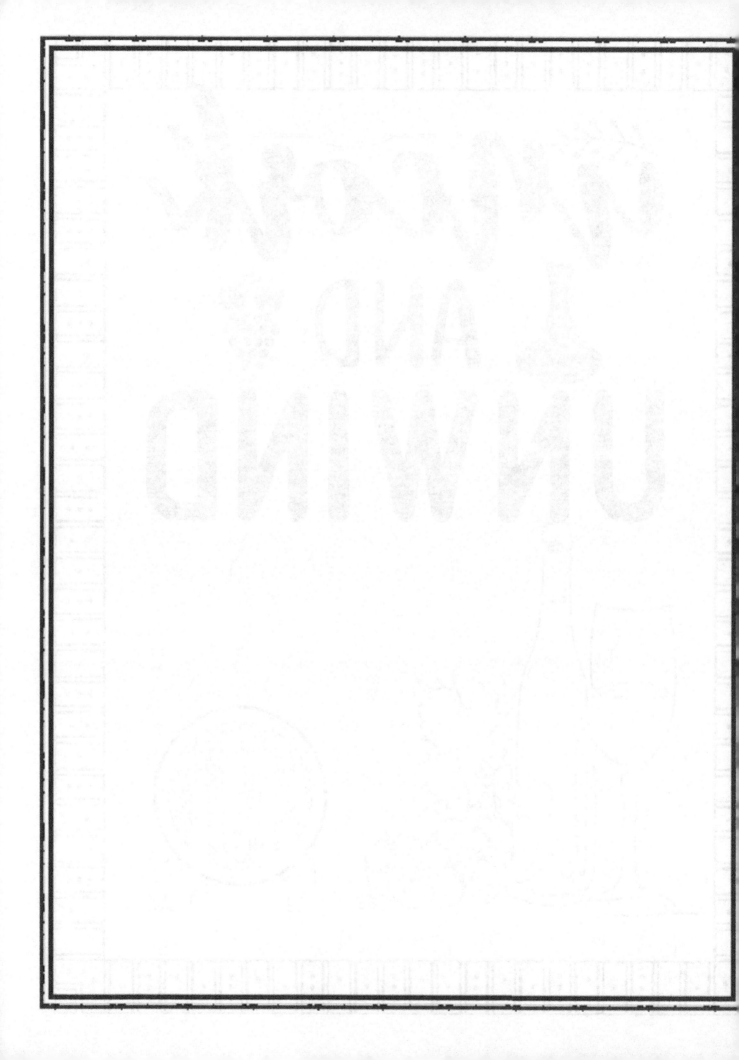

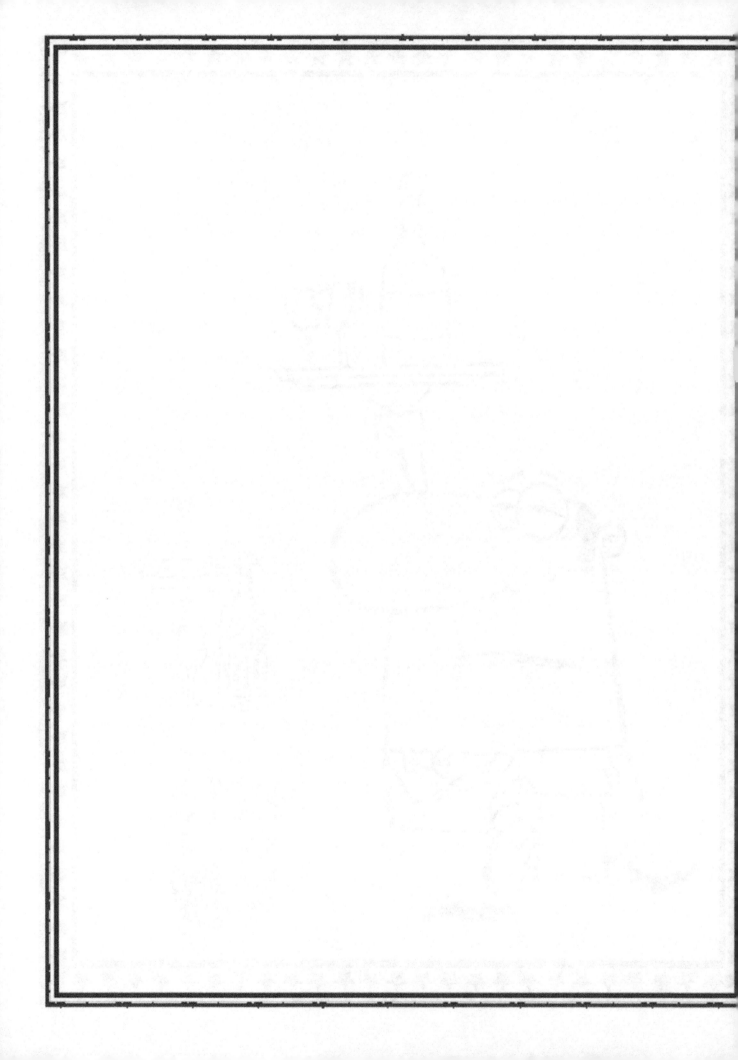

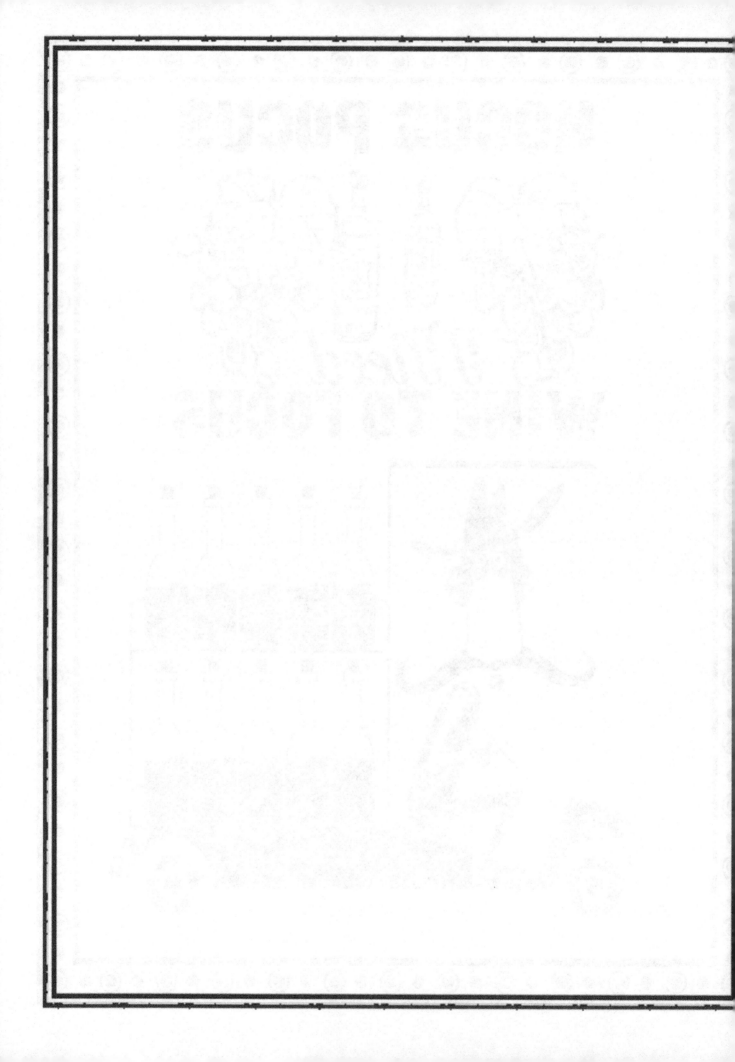

Made in the USA
Monee, IL
21 September 2023